Hockey

Julie Murray

Abdo
SPORTS HOW TO
Kids

abdopublishing.com

Published by Abdo Kids, a division of ABDO, P.O. Box 398166, Minneapolis, Minnesota 55439.
Copyright © 2018 by Abdo Consulting Group, Inc. International copyrights reserved in all countries.
No part of this book may be reproduced in any form without written permission from the publisher.
Abdo Kids Junior™ is a trademark and logo of Abdo Kids.

Printed in the United States of America, North Mankato, Minnesota.

102017

012018

 THIS BOOK CONTAINS
RECYCLED MATERIALS

Photo Credits: Alamy, Getty Images, iStock, Shutterstock

Production Contributors: Teddy Borth, Jennie Forsberg, Grace Hansen

Design Contributors: Christina Doffing, Candice Keimig, Dorothy Toth

Publisher's Cataloging-in-Publication Data

Names: Murray, Julie, author.

Title: Hockey / by Julie Murray.

Description: Minneapolis, Minnesota : Abdo Kids, 2018. | Series: Sports how to |
        Includes glossary, index and online resource (page 24).

Identifiers: LCCN 2017908187 | ISBN 9781532104152 (lib.bdg.) | ISBN 9781532105272 (ebook) |
        ISBN 9781532105838 (Read-to-me ebook)

Subjects: LCSH: Hockey--Juvenile literature. | Sports and recreation--Juvenile literature.

Classification: DDC 796.962 --dc23

LC record available at https://lccn.loc.gov/2017908187

Table of Contents

Hockey

Jon loves hockey! He is ready to play.

helmet

glove

pads

stick

ice skate

puck

5

Hockey is played on an ice rink.

Each team has 6 players.

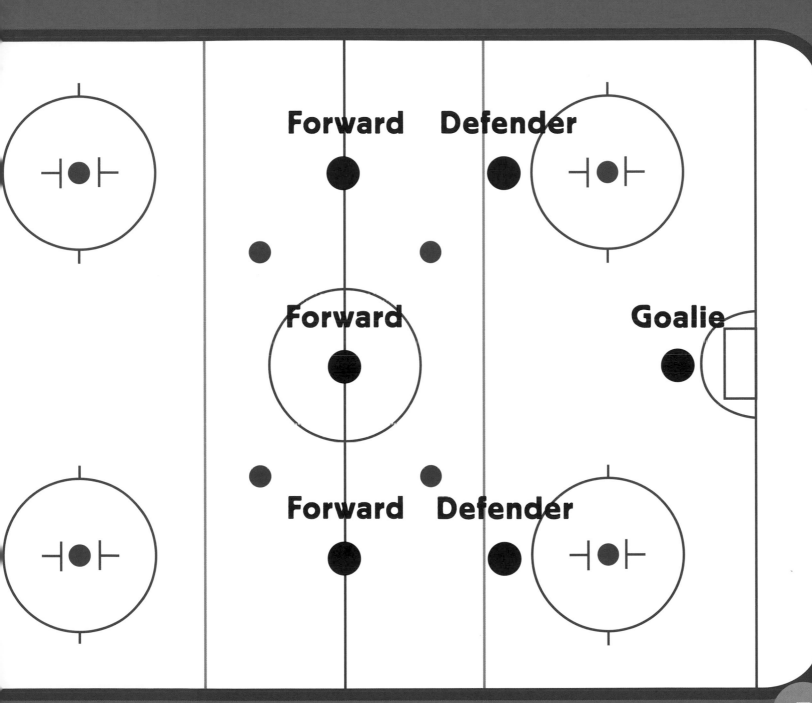

Forward Defender

Forward

Goalie

Forward Defender

The rink has 3 **zones**.

An **NHL** game is 60 minutes. There are 3 periods. Each one is 20 minutes.

One team tries to put the puck in the net. It is one point.

Two players are in a **face-off**.

Jim is fast. He gets the puck.

He passes it.

Elsa shoots. The goalie stops it.
She has special gear. This keeps
her safe.

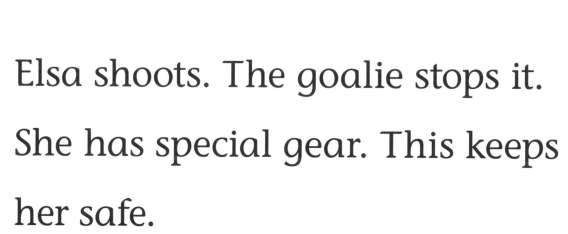

Ken broke a rule. He sits in the penalty box. After two minutes he can play again.

Jessica takes a shot. It goes in the net. She scores!

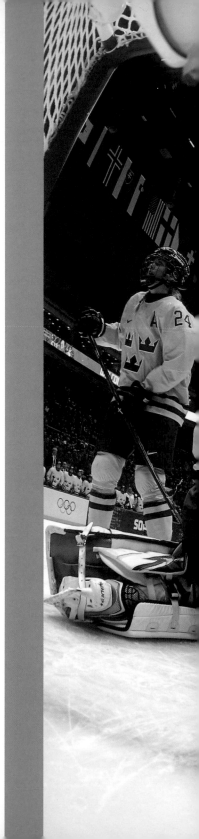

Some Features of a Hockey Rink

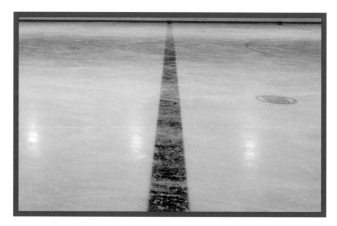
blue line

boards

face-off circle

goal crease

Glossary

NHL
short for National Hockey League.

face-off
the start of play where the referee drops the puck between two players on different teams.

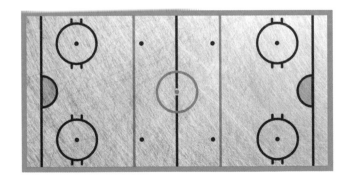

zone
one of three areas (defending, neutral, and attacking zones) on a rink divided by the blue lines.

Index

Abdo Kids
ONLINE
FREE! ONLINE MULTIMEDIA RESOURCES

Visit **abdokids.com** and use this code to access crafts, games, videos, and more!

Abdo Kids Code:
SHK4152